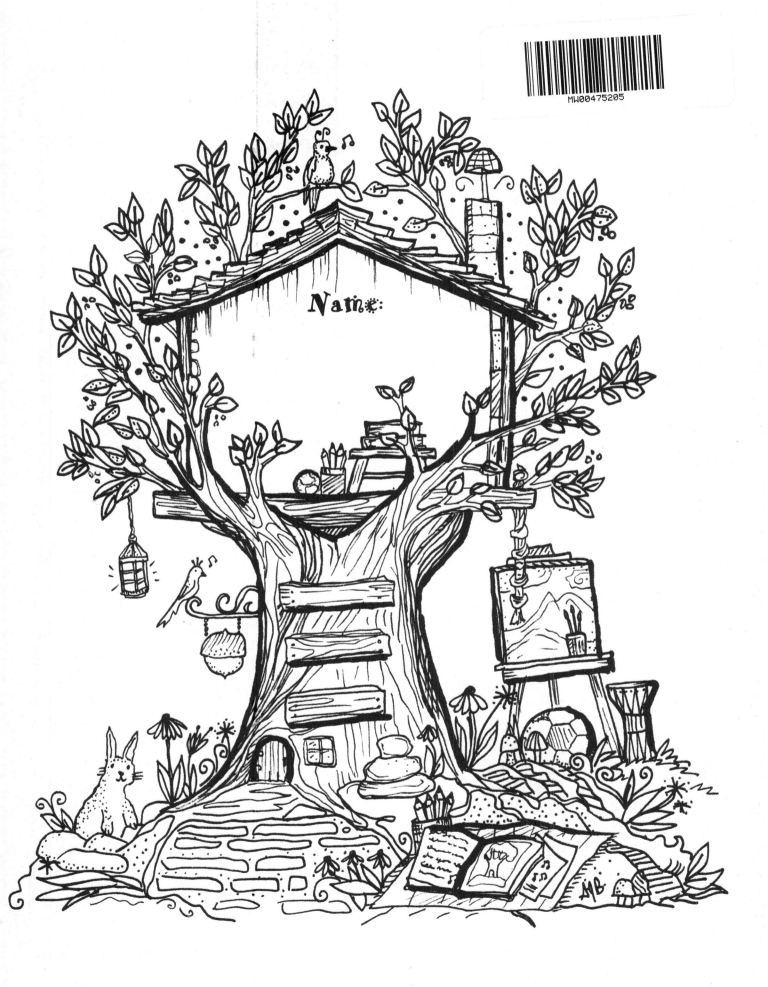

Name:

About the Past Times Newspaper Reporter's Journal

Have you ever wondered what it would be like to be an on-the-scene reporter for events throughout history? This is your chance. The Past Times Paper gives students the chance to get up close with history in a way nothing else does. In this unique journal, students become the reporter.

Building creative writing, research, and journalism skills students will create their own newspaper. We provide prompts and the newspaper template, students get to fill in the rest. They will create ads based on the time period, comic strips, newspaper games, artwork, and more.

This journal is perfect for budding journalists, writers, history buffs, and creative learners. It is a wonderful way to introduce students to history in a way that's fun and engaging- no dry textbooks and boring book reports here!

Use daily for an intensive History and Writing unit lasting about a month, or weekly to last all year. You can even use this over a period of several years as you study different periods in history.

Thinking Tree Learning Levels: B2, C1 & C2, ideal for ages 10+. Younger students with assistance.

How to Use This Book:

Research each event and tell the story in your own words as if you were a news reporter at the time the event was happening!

Be sure to use your imagination and include character interviews and quotes in your news story.

The Thinking Tree

Time Travel
American History

PAST TIMES NEWSPAPER

You be the
REPORTER

Anna Miriam Brown

Sarah Janisse Brown

Joshua William Brown

Article by:_ _ _ _ _ _ _ _ _ _ _ _ _ _ _ _

Date:_ _ _ 1492 AD _

Colombus Discovers New World

Christopher Colombus Discovers the West Indies

Be Creative

Be Creative

Weekly Games

Make your own Past Times Paper word search.

Words to Find:

Past Times Paper

Article by:_ _ _ _ _ _ _ _ _ _ _ _ _ _ _ _ _ _

Date:_ _ · 1621 _ _ _ _ _ _

Three-Day Celebration of Successful Harvest

The First "Thanksgiving"

Be Creative

Weekly Comic

Make a Past Times Paper comic strip

Past Times Paper

Article by:_ _ _ _ _ _ _ _ _ _ _ _ _ _ _ _

Date:_ _ 1752 _ _ _

B. Franklin Demonstrates Lightning is Electric

Benjamin Franklin and The Kite Experiment

Be Creative

Weekly Ad

Design a Past Times Paper advertisement based on the types of items sold during the time of your last article

Article by:_ _ _ _ _ _ _ _ _ _ _ _ _ _ _ _ _ _ _ _

Date:_ _ 1773 _ _ _ _

Enough! Tea Dumped Into Boston Harbor

Boston Tea Party

Be Creative

Weekly Games

Make your own Past Times Paper word search.

Words to Find:

_____   _____   _____

_____   _____   _____

_____   _____   _____

_____   _____   _____

_____   _____   _____

Article by:_ _ _ _ _ _ _ _ _ _ _ _ _ _ _ _ _   Date:_ _ 1776_ _ _ _ _ _

Independence from England Declared!

The Declaration of Independence

Be Creative

Be Creative

Weekly Comic

Make a Past Times Paper comic strip

Past Times Paper

Article by: _ _ _ _ _ _ _ _ _ _ _ _ _ _ _ _

Date: _ _ 1781 _ _ _ _

Independence from England Declared!

The Declaration of Independence

_____
_____
_____
_____
_____
_____
_____
_____
_____
_____
_____
_____
_____
_____
_____
_____
_____
_____
_____
_____
_____
_____
_____
_____
_____
_____
_____
_____
_____
_____
_____
_____

Be Creative

Weekly Ad

Design a Past Times Paper advertisement based on the types of items sold during the time of your last article

Past Times Paper

Article by:_   Date:_ _ _ 1791 _ _ _ _ _ _ _ _ _

Pennsylvania and the Whiskey Rebellion

Write your own headlines from now on!

Be Creative

Be Creative

Weekly Games

Make your own Past Times Paper word search.

Words to Find:

Past Times Paper

Article by:_ _ _ _ _ _ _ _ _ _ _ _ _ _ _ _ _

Date:_ _ _ 1797 _ _ _

President Washington Resigns

Be Creative

Be Creative

Weekly Comic

Make a Past Times Paper comic strip

Past Times Paper

Article by:_ _ _ _ _ _ _ _ _ _ _ _ _ _ _

Date:_ _ _ 1803 _ _ _ _

The Louisiana Purchase

Be Creative

Weekly Ad

Design a Past Times Paper advertisement based on the types of items sold during the time of your last article

Article by:_ _ _ _ _ _ _ _ _ _ _ _ _ _ _ _ _

Date:_ _ _ _ 1804 _ _ _

Alexander Hamilton's Death by Duel

Be Creative

Weekly Games

Make your own Past Times Paper word search.

Words to Find:

Past Times Paper

Article by:_ _ _ _ _ _ _ _ _ _ _ _ _ _ _ _ _ _

Date:_ _ _ _ 1806 _ _ _

New York's First Private Orphanage

Be Creative

Be Creative

Weekly Comic

Make a Past Times Paper comic strip

Past Times Paper

Article by:_ _ _ _ _ _ _ _ _ _ _ _ _ _ _ _ _

Date:_ _ _ 1815 _ _ _ _ _

Andrew Jackson Leads the Battle of New Orleans

Be Creative

Be Creative

Weekly Ad

Design a Past Times Paper advertisement based on the types of items sold during the time of your last article

Past Times Paper

Article by:_ _ _ _ _ _ _ _ _ _ _ _ _ _ _ _ _ _ _

Date:_ 1823 _ _ _ _ _ _ _ _ _

The Monroe Doctrine

Be Creative

Be Creative

Weekly Games

Make your own Past Times Paper word search.

Words to Find:

_____ _____ _____
_____ _____ _____
_____ _____ _____
_____ _____ _____
_____ _____ _____

Past Times Paper

Article by:_ _ _ _ _ _ _ _ _ _ _ _ _ _ _ _ _ _

Date:_ _ _ _ 1848 _ _ _ _

Signing of the Treaty of Guadalupe Hidalgo

Be Creative

Weekly Comic

Make a Past Times Paper comic strip

Past Times Paper

The Beginning of the Civil War

Be Creative

Weekly Ad

Design a Past Times Paper advertisement based on the types of
items sold during the time of your last article

Past Times Paper

Article by:_ _ _ _ _ _ _ _ _ _ _ _ _ _ _ _

The Abolishment of Slavery

Be Creative

Be Creative

Weekly Games

Make your own Past Times Paper word search.

Words to Find:

_____ _____ _____

_____ _____ _____

_____ _____ _____

_____ _____ _____

_____ _____ _____

Past Times Paper

Article by:_ _ _ _ _ _ _ _ _ _ _ _ _ _ _ _

Date:_ _ _ _ 1865_ _ _ _

The Assassination of Abraham Lincoln

Be Creative

Weekly Comic

Make a Past Times Paper comic strip

Past Times Paper

Article by:_ _ _ _ _ _ _ _ _ _ _ _ _ _ _ _   Date:_ _ _ _ _ _ _ _ _ _

The Peshtigo Fire

Be Creative

Be Creative

Weekly Ad

Design a Past Times Paper advertisement based on the types of
items sold during the time of your last article

Past Times Paper

Article by:_ _ _ _ _ _ _ _ _ _ _ _ _ _ _ _ _   Date:_ _ _ **1876** _ _ _

The Invention of the Telephone by Alexander Graham Bell

Be Creative

Weekly Games

Make your own Past Times Paper word search.

Words to Find:

_____   _____   _____
_____   _____   _____
_____   _____   _____
_____   _____   _____
_____   _____   _____
_____   _____   _____
_____   _____   _____

Past Times Paper

Article by:_ _ _ _ _ _ _ _ _ _ _ _ _ _ _ _ _ _

Date:_ _ _ _ _ _ _ _ _ 1879

Edison Invents the Light Bulb

Be Creative

Be Creative

Weekly Comic

Make a Past Times Paper comic strip

Past Times Paper

The Wright Brothers First Flight

Be Creative

Weekly Ad

Design a Past Times Paper advertisement based on the types of items sold during the time of your last article

Past Times Paper

Article by:_ _ _ _ _ _ _ _ _ _ _ _ _ _ _ _ _

Date:_ _ 1906 _ _ _ _ _

The Devastating San Francisco Earthquake

Be Creative

Be Creative

Weekly Games

Make your own Past Times Paper word search.

Words to Find:

_____ _____ _____

_____ _____ _____

_____ _____ _____

_____ _____ _____

_____ _____ _____

Past Times Paper

Article by:_ _ _ _ _ _ _ _ _ _ _ _ _ _ _ _ _

Date:_ _ _1912_ _ _ _ _

The Sinking of the Titanic

Be Creative

Weekly Comic

Make a Past Times Paper comic strip

Past Times Paper

Article by:_ _ _ _ _ _ _ _ _ _ _ _ _ _ _ _ _

Date:_ _ _ _ _ _ _ _ 1920

Women Granted Right to Vote

Be Creative

Be Creative

Weekly Ad

Design a Past Times Paper advertisement based on the types of items sold during the time of your last article

Past Times Paper

Article by:_ _ _ _ _ _ _ _ _ _ _ _ _ _ _ _ _ _ _

Date:_ _ _ _ _1929_ _ _ _

The Beginning of the Great Depression

Be Creative

Be Creative

Weekly Games

Make your own Past Times Paper word search.

Words to Find:

Past Times Paper

Article by:_ _ _ _ _ _ _ _ _ _ _ _ _ _ _ _

Date:_ _ 1941_ _ _ _ _ _

The Attack on Pearl Harbor

Be Creative

Be Creative

Weekly Comic

Make a Past Times Paper comic strip

Past Times Paper

Article by:_ _ _ _ _ _ _ _ _ _ _ _ _ _ _ _

Date:_ _ 1946 _ _ _ _

The Manhattan Project

Be Creative

Weekly Ad

Design a Past Times Paper advertisement based on the types of items sold during the time of your last article

Past Times Paper

Article by:_ _ _ _ _ _ _ _ _ _ _ _ _ _ _ _ _ _

Date:_ · 1955 _ _ _ _ _ _ _ _

Dr. Jonas Salk's Polio Vaccine Proven Effective

Be Creative

Be Creative

Weekly Games

Make your own Past Times Paper word search.

Words to Find:

Past Times Paper

First African-American Child Integrated into an All White School

Be Creative

Weekly Comic

Make a Past Times Paper comic strip

Past Times Paper

The Assassination of President John F. Kennedy

Be Creative

Weekly Ad

Design a Past Times Paper advertisement based on the types of items sold during the time of your last article

Past Times Paper

Article by:_ _ _ _ _ _ _ _ _ _ _ _ _ _ _ _

Date:_ _ _ 1968 _ _ _ _

The Assassination of Martin Luther King Jr.

Be Creative

Weekly Games

Make your own Past Times Paper word search.

Words to Find:

_____   _____   _____

_____   _____   _____

_____   _____   _____

_____   _____   _____

_____   _____   _____

Past Times Paper

First Man Walks on the Moon

Be Creative

Be Creative

Weekly Comic

Make a Past Times Paper comic strip

Past Times Paper

Article by:_ _ _ _ _ _ _ _ _ _ _ _ _ _ _ _ _ _

Date:_ _ _ _ 1972 _ _ _

The Watergate Scandal is Revealed

Be Creative

Weekly Ad

Design a Past Times Paper advertisement based on the types of items sold during the time of your last article

Past Times Paper

Article by:_ _ _ _ _ _ _ _ _ _ _ _ _ _ _

Date:_ _ _ _ 1981 _ _ _

NASA Launches STS-1

Be Creative

Be Creative

Weekly Games

Make your own Past Times Paper word search.

Words to Find:

_____ _____ _____
_____ _____ _____
_____ _____ _____
_____ _____ _____
_____ _____ _____
_____ _____ _____

Past Times Paper

Article by:_ _ _ _ _ _ _ _ _ _ _ _ _ _ _ _

Date:_ _ 1986 _ _ _ _ _

The Explosion of the Challenger Space Shuttle

Be Creative

Weekly Comic

Make a Past Times Paper comic strip

Past Times Paper

Article by:_ _ _ _ _ _ _ _ _ _ _ _ _ _ _ _ _ _

Date:_ _ _ 1987 _ _ _

The Rescue of Baby Jessica

Be Creative

Weekly Ad

Design a Past Times Paper advertisement based on the types of items sold during the time of your last article

Past Times Paper

Article by:_ _ _ _ _ _ _ _ _ _ _ _ _ _ _ _

Date:_ _ _ 1989 _ _ _ _

The Exxon Valdez Oil Spill

Be Creative

Be Creative

Weekly Games

Make your own Past Times Paper word search.

Words to Find:

Past Times Paper

Article by:_ _ _ _ _ _ _ _ _ _ _ _ _ _ _ _ _ _ _

Date:_ _ _ _ 1999 _ _ _

The Columbine Tragedy

Be Creative

Weekly Comic

Make a Past Times Paper comic strip

Past Times Paper

September 11, 2001

Be Creative

𝔚eekly 𝔄d

Design a Past Times Paper advertisement based on the types of items sold during the time of your last article

Past Times Paper

Article by:_ _ _ _ _ _ _ _ _ _ _ _ _ _ _ _ _ _ _

Date:_ _ _ 2004 _ _ _

Bob and Vint Create "The Internet"

Be Creative

𝔚eekly 𝔊ames

Make your own Past Times Paper word search.

Words to Find:

_____ _____ _____
_____ _____ _____
_____ _____ _____
_____ _____ _____
_____ _____ _____
_____ _____ _____

Past Times Paper

The Devastation of Hurricane Katrina

Be Creative

Weekly Comic

Make a Past Times Paper comic strip

Past Times Paper

Article by:_ _ _ _ _ _ _ _ _ _ _ _ _ _ _ _

Date:_ _ _ 2007 _ _ _ _

The Announcement of the Original iphone

Be Creative

Weekly Ad

Design a Past Times Paper advertisement based on the types of
items sold during the time of your last article

Past Times Paper

Article by:_ _ _ _ _ _ _ _ _ _ _ _ _ _ _ _ _

Date:_ _ _ **2008**_ _ _ _

The Election of the First African-American President

Be Creative

Weekly Games

Make your own Past Times Paper word search.

Words to Find:

Past Times Paper

Article by:_ _ _ _ _ _ _ _ _ _ _ _ _ _ _ _

Date:_ _ 2010 _ _ _ _

Elon Musk Announces Another Genius Invention

Be Creative

Weekly Comic

Make a Past Times Paper comic strip

Past Times Paper

Article by:_ _ _ _ _ _ _ _ _ _ _ _ _ _ _ _ _ _   Date:_ _ _ _ _ _ _ _ _ _

Choose your own event in history to write about.

Be Creative

Weekly Comic

Make a Past Times Paper comic strip

Past Times Paper

Article by:_ _ _ _ _ _ _ _ _ _ _ _ _ _ _   Date:_ _ _ _ _ _ _ _

Choose your own event in American history to write about.

Past Times Paper

Article by:_____

Date:_____

Choose your own event in American history to write about.

Be Creative

Weekly Comic

Make a Past Times Paper comic strip

Be Creative

Be Creative

Weekly Comic

Make a Past Times Paper comic strip

What Is Fun-Schooling?

Fun-schooling is a one-of-a-kind way to learn. It is tapping into kids' interests while covering all the major subjects. Fun-schooling is for creative learners, students with learning disabilities, gifted students, and everyone in between. It's a way for students to learn without the stress, pressure, and boredom of other methods. We started out creating materials for our children. Then friends and family wanted to try it out. Before we knew it, Fun-schooling with Thinking Tree Books was born!

Fun-Schooling With Thinking Tree Books

Contact Us:

The Thinking Tree LLC
+1 (USA)   317.622.8852

info@funschooling.com

THE THINKING TREE

FunSchooling.com

Made in the USA
Monee, IL
14 December 2021